TWELVE UNIVERSAL LAWS

OTHER BOOKS BY ANNE ANGELHEART

Awaken the Secret Within

TWELVE UNIVERSAL LAWS

The Truth That Will Transform Your Life

ANNE E. ANGELHEART

BALBOA.
PRESS

A DIVISION OF HAY HOUSE

Balboa Press books may be ordered through booksellers or by contacting:

Balboa Press
A Division of Hay House
1663 Liberty Drive
Bloomington, IN 47403
www.balboapress.com
1-(877) 407-4847

Because of the dynamic nature of the Internet, any web addresses or links contained in this book may have changed since publication and may no longer be valid. The views expressed in this work are solely those of the author and do not necessarily reflect the views of the publisher, and the publisher hereby disclaims any responsibility for them.

The author of this book does not dispense medical advice or prescribe the use of any technique as a form of treatment for physical, emotional, or medical problems without the advice of a physician, either directly or indirectly. The intent of the author is only to offer information of a general nature to help you in your quest for emotional and spiritual well-being. In the event you use any of the information in this book for yourself, which is your constitutional right, the author and the publisher assume no responsibility for your actions.

Any people depicted in stock imagery provided by Thinkstock are models, and such images are being used for illustrative purposes only.
Certain stock imagery © Thinkstock.

ISBN: 978-1-4525-3698-9 (e)
ISBN: 978-1-4525-3697-2 (sc)

Printed in the United States of America

Balboa Press rev. date: 7/29/2011

CONTENTS

ACKNOWLEDGEMENTS

This book has been long awaited for. This is the information I have always wanted to share with others as when I walked with my teachers here. I know the enormous impact and change it has made in my life. I am excited and my heart is full of gratitude to have all the people in my life who have encouraged me or somehow assisted me to get this word out to the world.

I want to thank all of my teachers in this walking journey called life and their patience with me as I was one stubborn student. I thank all I have met on the journey that I have actively learned these lessons through my experiences with them here. I thank all of my students and clients who forever continue to challenge me and stretch me to grow.

I want to thank all of my students or clients who have physically in some way assisted us with this work to getting the product finished and in the physical. Although I do not personally know my editor, Lynda Forman, I thank her. I appreciate and recognize her talent and know we would not have this product without her.

A special thanks to my daughter, Naomi Christianson, who works so very hard to get all of the work I do out to the world with her creativity and great tenacity. Jennifer Munguia has been a great help to keep me sane by taking care of details I would rather not add to my plate and making things run smoothly. Thanks to Gillian Ceja for doing so much work in research, posting, and submitting my work all over since I would not have the time to do this. I thank all of them from the deepest part of my heart for they are blessings beyond words.

I thank all who have continued to ask me to create new projects and books and believe in the work.

Blessings,
Anne Angelheart

INTRODUCTION

Can you feel it? Can you feel the stirrings of your heart and Soul? Do you feel it deep within your core: an unexplained deep desire to heal, transform, release old personal, cultural, familial and ancestral patterns on all levels once and for all so that you may truly be free to BE and express the Soul Essence of who you REALLY are?

More and more people everyday are awakening to the clarity that old ways of being no longer serve them, or the Earth, and they sense a new way of Be-ing that resonates with their Soul. Some may choose to be guided by their senses and therefore take a more joyful path and flow freely in the higher vibrations of this New Consciousness. Others may choose a more resistant path and feel themselves in the rapids of this flow. There is neither a wrong nor a right way to shift into this New Consciousness, just a more joyful or less joyful way.

I encourage you to feel and embrace this time of great change, healing, purification, and transformation. Allow the awakening of your True Heart, your True Being and Essence, your memory of ALL that YOU are. Take this time and utilize that "stirring" feeling deep within- transforming that energy into excitement, new-ness, passion, and creation. Do not let it linger and transmute into fear, anxiety, and survival. Surely you would want to use this fork in the road of consciousness at this accelerated time of change to choose the most joyful, transforming, all-that-you-can-be path.

There are many tools and resources for you to utilize on your path during this shift in consciousness. This book is one of them which tells me that if you have been drawn to Universal Laws, you are sensing a new way of being that resonates with your Soul.

This book includes all 12 Universal Laws and provides identification and integration of them into your daily living. By using new language, relatable examples, and experiences, you will immediately feel your connection to these ancient concepts and will be able to remember how to apply them in your life on a regular basis rather than selectively.

Whether you are conscious of it or not, Universal Laws are making an impact on your life, so again, use this time of awakening to take charge of your journey and remember you are the Creator of your life.

THE LAW OF ONENESS

What is the Place of Oneness?

Many of us have been taught that Oneness is when we tune into others or nature and become one with the world, yet it is much more than that. It is actually FEELING and knowing that we are all connected to all things, people, animals, and nature. Beyond that, we are one with the universe, knowing and feeling how we all started from the ONE and are all a fragment of the One.

A Concept of Creation

One concept of creation was there was Source, the ALL THAT IS! Energy, this consciousness sent out a sound and that sound returned to Itself. When it returned to itself, it sent out another sound in answer to it. Each sound was a specific tone or frequency. As it traveled and returned each time it changed frequency. Each frequency manifested its sound into light, each light is over soul. After many frequencies had been manifested into light, these lights became a consciousness of its own and we will call them all Over Soul.

Each Over Soul split into two rays of light. One ray was silver and one was gold. Each of these we will now call Soul. Each Soul started to create planets and began to incarnate on them. In actuality, all time and lifetimes are actually happening simultaneously. So each soul which was incarnated in many dimensions and time periods simultaneously these lights were extensions of each soul, which we will call spirit.

Our linear minds have to call them past lives and future lives for the human mind to understand. This is why when you visit a past or future life and you make a change while visiting it whether in meditation or hypnotherapy, when you make a change there you feel a change in your here and now. The reason is because they are all happening simultaneously.

Since we all began from Source and we all co-created all there is right now that is in existence then we are all One and connected.

Why The Place Of Oneness is Different Than Our Concept of One with All

Through the teachings of the New Age and meditations, we were taught to go out and become one with nature, a tree, or an animal. This is not oneness this is consciously connecting to another. We are always connected, but this is consciously connecting. We are already one with all so when we are taught we have to tune in and become one, this is not the truth.

<u>We are always connected.</u>

When we are doing this exercise of tuning into a plant or animal, we are just putting our consciousness (attention) on connecting so we feel we have connected and became one. If we are always already connected we are just being aware of it in these moments. If we believe meditating on being one with all on the planet and that is what connects us as One, then we are limiting our selves. To know we are carrying and being the oneness from inside then we are unlimited.

We are not simply observers of the world around us or the energies around us — we are a part of this universe, a crucial part. When we can recognize that we are One, we can see how our actions impact others.

But it's not just a matter of noticing and thinking about the idea of being one with everything.

There is a big difference in being aware and conscious of being Oneness compared to becoming one with a limited aspect here in the earthly space. You would have felt a difference in the meditation.

While everyone's experience will be different, as experiences continue to be limited or altered by the experiences we've had before, when you tap into being One, instead of being aware of one, you will notice that things are bigger.

This feeling can be compared to the idea of wanting a child and having a child. The idea of becoming a parent is something you can only understand at a certain level, until you are actually within the experience. And even though you can talk to others about this experience, they will not understand unless they too become a parent.

People also look for the feeling of unconditional love when they are consciously revisiting the place of Oneness. They look for feeling of euphoria and burst of energy or something similar. In all reality, Oneness is just energy and does not have all of these feelings. Feelings belong to the body and are felt based on our belief systems. To visit the true place of Oneness, it is a place and feeling of it just Is — there is no part of it that is created by our experiences or beliefs. If you have thoughts or emotions occurring while you are focusing on Oneness, then you are not in the true place of Oneness. There are many levels of Oneness, so I am only talking about the original place of Oneness where everything began.

How Does This Apply to Now?

Once we started to incarnate, we labeled things and those labels changed meaning as linear time went on. Whatever we had labeled, we then created belief systems around them. Now the world reflects to us through our labeling our belief systems. This language became tools to communicate with self and other spirits on the planet. This is why if you studied about power animal and totems, we put a belief system to them of what they mean. Now when one of these animals comes to us, we base our message on the labeled belief we have of what that animal means. A tool to talk to our own spirit. These tools are okay and work, but if we were conscious of the place of Oneness, we would not need these tools to be used to hear Source within us. Since we originated from Source, it is our own self answering us. This is where the esoteric teaching came from of all the answers are inside of us: your own teacher is within.

Another teaching that keeps us separate from embracing Oneness is that we subtly continue to create separateness and disconnectedness. Many teachings tell us to disconnect from negativity, disconnect from a person or situation that is not healthy for us. In reality, it is impossible to disconnect, since we are all the same energy of Oneness. If you want to open more to the ONE then you may want to say, *I transmute this energy* NOT disconnect.

Whatever you believe IS SO! If you are using words all day saying *disconnect from this, from that,* you are actually saying disconnect from a part of yourself, which is all part of the ONE, Source. We end up creating more separateness from the One so subtly throughout our day, we are not aware of doing this.

Examples

Many times as healers and teachers we are doing the healing work through readings or sending healing energies to someone. We send energy and we read information that belongs to the other person. Yet, we say, "I can't seem to transmute my thoughts," or "I can't get this information for myself."

It's interesting that so many healers find themselves in this position. Though it might seem impossible, those who are more aware of energies will often find themselves overwhelmed by what they can feel.

It's almost as if you are so open to everything that you can't process it all. And the truth is that the human mind can't process everything. There are limits until you can be in the state of Oneness. Even then, you are limited in how you can share that with others. Words are meaningless in these cases.

You can access any energy you like, but handing this over to a client can become challenging.

If you understand the One, you have to ask, "If I can access it to get others information, why can't I get mine?" Ask yourself, "If I can transmute energy and send healing to others and I cannot transmute my own thoughts?" Something to think about for this is what we are putting out in the universe and it is one of the ways we create more separateness from the One.

By accessing Oneness, you begin to see that all energy is connected. If you can access energy for your clients, then you can access energy for yourself.

Perhaps your focus on 'getting' something for your clients informs the way that you draw energy to yourself. Since your clients expect you to bring something to them, you attract what they need.

But since you may be more hesitant to do this for yourself, you might not be open to Oneness for yourself. In this case, you want to focus your mind on creating positive thoughts and the confidence that you can access energies for yourself.

You already know you can, after all. Accessing one person's energy has already proven this to be the case.

Another example is believing we only feel the oneness when we meditate or are in nature. Then you are creating the concept and a truth for yourself that you are NOT connected and aware of Oneness throughout your everyday.

You actually can't detach from Oneness. You might not have a stronger experience of this state in some places in your life, but it is impossible to detach from Oneness as it is everything.

When you start to look at this state in that way, you begin to see that there is no escaping the very thing you're seeking. Instead of looking at this process as a chase, think of this process and this experience as something you merely want to open to.

By opening up to Oneness, you can invite it into your life, where it can become a permanent houseguest.

Many of us are disconnected because of the way we live our lives and the way that society tells us to live our lives.

For example, societal labels create beliefs and beliefs are what create separateness. The universal laws are just what energy IS; energy does not become anything until we label it and create our belief systems. Our belief systems create separateness and limitations. We think that we believe this and all THAT is not a part of the belief system, so it needs to be discarded.

Instead, it can be more effective to think about your life in terms of ideas. The ideas you have are always accepted, even when beliefs are argued or dismissed by others. Simply reframing the way you look at your life can create the space in which you can be one with everything around you.

Ideas are also not labels. They're more nebulous categories that can be moved and shifted.

Remember Source is energy and what we label and believe with energy is an expression of Source. All is One until we manifest it and now it is an expression of Source, our expression. At the same time, these labels can limit us, if we allow them to.

We become unlimited when we truly understand the ONE and we are conscious that we are choosing how we want to express Source. There are no labels in the universe, after all. We are the ones doing that work.

The universe just IS.

You may not grasp this concept all at once, so be patient with yourself. You have already created layers and layers of belief systems even from other lifetimes. With each layer you remove, the deeper you will understand this law. As we move onto the other laws, we must not stop applying the previous laws, as they all interact with each other. As we add the other laws, it will allow this one to become clearer.

Law One Exercises

Exercise One
Get in a comfortable position and take a few deep breaths. Release all tensions of the day and breathe until your whole body is relaxed.

After you are completely relaxed, ask your own soul or ask for assistance from a guide to go to what we will call the sea of love, _____, to the place of Oneness before all was created. When you reach this place, you will feel as though there is nothing, yet you will feel it is the place of everything.

Feel how this oneness feels, is there sound? Is there color? Are there senses? Spend about ten minutes exploring what this oneness feels like. Notice the difference between this feeling of oneness and when you say you are one with all on the planet.

Note: If you find you are having thoughts in this place, you are not at Oneness. Ask again to go to Oneness before all was created. If you see colors, you are not there; if you are seeing things as if on a journey you are not there. This is NOT a place to ask questions or a space to find answers to questions; It JUST IS, so just experience it.

Exercise Two
Buy some play dough. Put the dough in a ball and sit for a minute and see it as All One. We will have it symbolize Source. Now take a pinch from the dough and with small amounts, making each of these miniatures, form the dough into a:

Cup
Plate
Bowl
Flower
An animal

Look at this and contemplate how it all came from the one, yet once it was shaped and labeled it became individual, it took on a different feeling of energy. Yet, it is still all from the same source. Now contemplate how all on this planet, in the universe, is the same as this.

You may think to yourself, I already get the concept so I don't need to do the actual exercise. Not true, when we do an action and use our body in this action, it assists to embrace the concept on a deeper and core level.

Exercise Three
Apply all that you have learned in this chapter today and stay conscious throughout your day. Allow yourself to see how it fits in all we do, say and experience daily on a conscious level.

Journal what ways you see and experience the world differently applying the concept of Oneness to daily conscious living.

THE LAW OF ENERGY OR VIBRATION

The law of energy or vibration shows us that everything attracts or repels other energies in the environment. It shows us how energy or vibration is a frequency and it broadcasts throughout our everyday lives.

To understand this we want to know what our own frequency is. We are not talking about the aura of the body, which is different. An aura is the subtle energy field around the body, but one's frequency is just a part of that aura. Many frequencies in the aura are created by our thoughts and our wants.

Think about this as a radio. There is one radio, but many stations on this radio to which you can turn to have different experiences.

Each of us has a frequency unique to our self, the vibration of our soul. This frequency broadcasts throughout the universe. This is how a soul family, no matter where they are on the planet, will find you. The more conscious we are of that frequency, the more we can gravitate soul family and contracts to us.

A Short Meditation on Hearing or/and Feeling Our Own Frequency

(This will not include our whole frequency as that would include our walk here and our aura. We want just the soul frequency.)

Close your eyes and take several deep cleansing breaths. As you breathe in, take in pure light and exhale any stress, worries, or anything on your mind. Do this until your body feels relaxed and your mind is quiet.

Then once you are relaxed ask yourself to hear your own frequency tone. This might be a sound, an image, or some other experience. You are the only one who can define what this experience might be and how it might manifest during your meditation. What you want to do is to just be open to the experience you have, trusting that anything you experience is right for you and something that you should hold to be true for your body at this time.

NOTE: Don't worry if it doesn't happen the first time, just keep doing this until you do.

Once you hear a tone or feel your frequency, sit with it for a moment so you will be able to recognize this sound or feeling. Then gently open your eyes, wiggle your toes, and feel present.

Once we discover where our vibration frequency is we can tune into a frequency as desired, like a radio wave and we tune our radio station into the one we choose. We will return to this later.

Energy/Frequency

Energy = makes up everything in the universe, there is nothing that is not made up of energy.

Vibration = a movement of energy, and energy is always moving.

Together, they bring our energy which is what we are with the vibration or movement that we make into our thoughts. The two combined are what becomes the movement that will manifest our thoughts into the physical realms.

Unclear thoughts = When our thoughts are unclear or scattered, the vibration you are attracting is unclear and the return will also be unclear. In this case instead of you tuning into a frequency you are tuning into whatever your thoughts bring to you. It is like instead of tuning into a clear radio station of music you like, you are on scan of the stations and you are being tuned into several static stations.

The goal is to gain clarity of thought and when you have this, the faster and easier it is to tune into the frequency you choose and want to bring to you. What does this mean? Clearing your mind and working on how you focus your thoughts is something many people realize, at some level, they need to do.

Think about a time when you were overwhelmed. In that time, when you were trying to center your thoughts, your life around you may have seemed out of control. While the overwhelmed state may have seemed to be caused by your life seeming out of control, the same could be said in reverse.

When you allowed your frequency to be tuned to the experience of being out of control, you attracted those situations that led you to be overwhelmed.

In order to start a new experience, you want to be able to stop and listen to your own thoughts, feeling for the vibrations you are attracting and then change your frequency to change your experience.

Instead of thinking about the way your life is out of control, consider the situation to be a process in which you can challenge yourself. If you look at the period as a challenge, you begin to see that you are focusing on the way that you can overcome your struggles, not on the struggles themselves.

Just like a radio, just a slight shift in frequency can lead to new music in your life.

How do we change frequency? We do this by changing our thoughts. It is not enough to change the thought in your mind only. It must have emotion, so feel the thought. Thought creates and emotion puts the thought in motion. This movement is what manifests the change.

You cannot simply say that you don't want to be overwhelmed anymore. You want to feel what it's like to be calm and immerse yourself in that feeling. When you tap into that frequency, you create the opportunity for your mind to be in line with the proper frequency.

That will lead you into a more positive experience for your life, depending on what you want from your life at this point.

How Does This Apply to Now?

Since everything is energy, including thought, we react to energies that are happening around us. If we walk into a room and many people are tense, we feel it before someone has verbally told us that a tense situation has occurred. If we walk around being moved by everyone's energy, this energy is controlling us and it is determining how we feel instead of us allowing us to choose how we want to feel. Randomly feeling all around us and reacting to it is flowing against the flow of the universe.

Recognizing the feeling and choosing to feel differently is action not reaction and then we are flowing with the universal law of vibration. When we are being active in the way we engage energy, we begin to vibrate differently, which allows the energy around us to vibrate differently.

Think of the pond that is smooth and glassy. It only changes that appearance when you poke a finger and create ripples. Just one small movement sends the entire pond into a new state.

And then those ripples create new ripples, which create new ripples...

These changes are brought about because of the action you took, not because you responded to the water. You CHOOSE to change the energy around you and this allows you to see changes in your life.

If you were to respond to the stillness of the water, you might not have touched the pond and nothing would have happened. Or you might have splashed the water that might have caused the pond to have less water in it, etc.

When you are the one who takes the action, the results you see are the ones that impact you in the way you want them to be impactful. You can change your frequency in order to create impact.

Remember how in the earlier meditation, we felt or began to feel our Soul vibration/frequency? Now that we know what it feels like, we can consciously choose to go to that frequency. So consciously we shift our self in that moment to our soul frequency. This will assist you into seeing the situation through the eyes of soul, which would mean a neutral viewpoint. Not unfeeling, the neutral meaning from the perspective of soul which has no judgment and it is from wisdom and understanding.

Walking in Soul

The next time you walk into a place or situation that does not feel comfortable, tell yourself to go to Soul frequency or go to neutral. Notice how much more understanding and wisdom you have for the situation or person at hand. Write about these experiences in your journal, you will see growth from doing this.

Going into neutral also assists us to be around others without being an uncomfortable energy for them. It assists us to find a new way to dance with each other. If someone is bothered by your energy, it does not mean you are not meant to work together. It is a lesson in how can we dance this dance of life together and enhance each other. Being in Soul provides new and unlimited experiences for all.

Make sure your energy is a clear frequency by having clarity in thought and questions. If you do not then your answers will return with the same lack of clarity or static. Pay attention if you are putting frequencies out in the day that is clear and with direct focus.

What Frequencies are We Sending Out into the World?

Many people believe if we are being conscious of what we are sending out, they can just send love or a positive energy out and it will change everything. This is a misconception. Thought alone will not send that transmutation of vibration out. It must have feeling behind it in order to move out into the world and actually manifest transmutation. You must truly own and feel the thought.

Another way we send out frequencies is with intent to change a situation or the feeling of another person. Again, if we think we can just send love, and it will work to create love, this is not true. If someone has issues that block them from feeling love or receiving love and they have a belief they do not deserve love, then if you label the energy "sent love," they may still have a negative reaction to it. It will not be interpreted by them when they feel the energy as the energy of love but instead as a frequency that is irritating and not what they want to receive. This can make them act out in an even more negative way.

The idea of changing your frequency does not necessarily mean that you are changing things to the way you want them to be. What you are doing, instead is adjusting your frequency to be more accepting of like energies around you.

This doesn't mean that you will always attract love when you send off love, but you will be more likely to. Everyone and everything has their own energy, and they have the same power that you have to adjust their energy when they feel the need.

You can only change yourself. You can only change your own frequency.

Examples

Once in a class I taught, we all picked a label out of a bowl and then proceeded to send that energy labeled on the paper to one person. Surprisingly, we were sending love to a student in the class and she perceived the energy as an attack.

Another time we were sending calm to one student, and each person focused intensely on his or her idea of calm. One student pictured a boat rocking on the ocean in a sunset scene. The receiver of this energy said she felt sick and nauseated. We later found out she was prone to motion sickness whenever she is in a boat.

We have good intentions when we believe we are sending out positive energy, but we are being in Ego to think we know what is best for someone. The receiver can only interpret the energy received according to their belief system.

Next time you send peace to a war, think about that. Do you think peace was a reality for someone like Hitler? He could have perceived that energy coming at him as an attack and escalated his anger and fury.

How do we send energy and see results? Practice sending energy by saying the intention is to send whatever that person or place wants for their own highest good. In this way, we are coming from the true heart and from Soul's perception, without judgment and no ego that we know what is best for others and allowing them to have their experiences as they want to for their own soul lessons.

Positive Frequencies

Positive frequencies can be perceived differently, and when they are, they will be interpreted by the receiver.

I played a crystal heart chakra bowl and asked the students what they felt. One said heart and one said root and they felt grounded. One said they felt it in solar plexus and heavy.

I then played the Mother's heartbeat on a drum and one said she felt rooted, one felt it in solar plexus, and one said made their stomach feel nervous and upset.

Heartbeat was played, but in two different frequencies and their belief systems were incorporated in their interpretation and perceptions. The woman, who felt heavy and sick to her stomach, had always been told she was everyone's mother and was an over giver. She had worked through not doing that, but she had a fear of overdoing it in an unhealthy way again. Even though she did not know what the sound represented, it hit her and made her feel uncomfortable.

Those that give so much of themselves often feel their own heart breaking when others try to tap into their heart's energy. Their hearts are so heavy with the weight of the world; they are more sensitive to the heart energies.

Even those, like this client, who have moved past the actions that sought to hold their light back, the energy is still present. No energy is ever destroyed.

Then I played a rattle and played a sound that is used to clear the energy field.

One student felt a psychic shower, one popped out of body, and one said, "I don't like that at all." It does not mean she did not want to clear the energy, it means that frequency does not resonate with her for clearing. The one that popped out of body, she said she always listens to rattles when taking a journey. The one in neutral felt what the rattling was meant for clearing the field.

All of these instruments emitted positive and high energies, but were received in different ways. Not all people felt them as comfortable and helpful energies. This is the same in everyday life. Just because we do not like someone's energy does not make it low or negative. Also, our high energy can feel as uncomfortable to someone with lower energy just as we feel uncomfortable with their energy. It is just because it is out of our comfort zone, different than what we know inside.

If we go to soul frequency or neutral, we will just know others as energy and be able to understand them better. This also makes us conscious and accountable for what we are sending out. Do not assume a high vibration being sent to someone is for their highest good or that you know which high vibration to send to them. Instead ask to send whatever is for their highest good, and it will never be uncomfortable or misinterpreted by the receiver.

Practice going to your Soul frequency and pay attention to the difference. Send whatever is of the highest good to others and note the difference.

Pay attention to everything and everyone you encounter as frequency and see what difference that makes in your daily walk.

Pay attention to what you are emanating, static, and unclear frequencies or clear and focused frequencies. You will receive back what you have broadcasted out.

Meditate and see yourself as a satellite dish sending and receiving transmissions from the earth and all on that the earth. What channels are you tuned into?

Remember from the previous oneness law that you live according to what you believe. You put energy out that way and you receive information that way. If you are in neutral, you will gain abundance of joy from the clarity of soul and from the place of no preconceived beliefs.

To ground this idea in a more relatable example, think about how a jury is picked for a trial. They are picked for their objectivity. If they cannot be objective, they might side with a certain lawyer because of their experience, not because of the unbiased evidence that is offered.

In the same way, when you create a place of neutrality, you create the space in which you can receive information and abundance. You aren't blocking joy from your life; you aren't hindered by beliefs that may no longer serve you.

Law Two Exercises

Exercise One
We felt earlier in this chapter in the meditation on what your frequency is and where you would like it to be. For the next two weeks, I want you to pay attention to the frequency of people around you.

Remember, if your frequency is higher, they can choose to raise theirs. But if they choose not to do so, they will feel your frequency just as irritating to them as theirs feels to you.

Find a neutral frequency to tune yourself into for the moment. Play with it, like a dial on a radio, choose different frequencies until you notice the other person and yourself feel more comfortable.

Exercise Two

The second week, pay attention to what situations you find yourself engaged in. Pay attention to what is being attracted to you and look at the situation as a frequency. Reflect how you might have called/attracted this frequency to you. At the same time, notice what energies you have repelled.

Once you become aware of your energy, practice changing your frequency every day and see what you attract on a daily basis.

Exercise Three

Put different music on for 2 different days and see how the frequency of each different type of music affects your frequency.

Exercise Four

Pay attention to everything in life this week as frequency, but combine this with what you learned about Oneness. They go together. Look around your life to see what the frequency is of things you do, thoughts you have, the way people respond to you, etc. Simply notice the idea of frequency. The more you look the more sensitive you will become.

THE LAW OF ACTION

The law of action must be applied in order for us to manifest things on earth. Therefore, we must engage in actions that support thoughts, dreams, emotions and words.

The law of action is simple, yet the least understood. This law means you want to move within the world consciously, planting seeds that will provide results for the things you truly want.

These actions can be as simple as reading about things you love or have passion for. They could be studying things you may want to do later in life or talking about what you have already learned in life to assist another in moving forward in their life. Action is taking part in life and to do this, you want to be giving and to be open to receiving.

Practicing or Teaching

Taking action is more than talking about what you have learned. Action is actually going out and practicing or teaching what you have learned. An example of this may be that you went through a divorce and experienced finding easier and better ways to process the action. You then shared this experience with others so they might use that information to walk more joyfully and informed in their own relationship challenges.

You may also have done research about nutrition so that you and your family could live a healthier lifestyle and then shared that research with others. This is another example of action in teaching what you have learned in life.

Taking Steps

You utilize the law of action when you take those steps in teaching. But just taking action is not enough; you want to follow through to the completion of your own goal or quest if you are to successfully integrate the law of action into your life.

Taking action requires a change in the way you are walking in your life. This change is twofold: a commitment on your part to learn with the thoughts of teaching, and a change in your normal behavior.

You must start walking (teaching) by making change in your behavior. If someone says something to you and it is mean and you react and retaliate with a mean comment, then you are taking an action in a lower frequency. You must be conscious and learn to take positive actions in all situations. Many think action is only necessary when they have a goal in life, such as a dream. They may make a vision board and meditate and do affirmations for this dream, but then they are taking action in other areas of life that are low frequency. As a result, they are still attracting low frequency and will not manifest what they truly want in that larger dream.

Sometimes just stopping your normal behaviors is a form of action. Many times we move through life with the same actions or reactions. What this does is stop us from the law of action to be applied with a successful result.

Many times we trick ourselves into believing and devising clever ways to react or to avoid situations or problems and justify these decisions. We trick ourselves into making these actions seem rational. Again, this stops us from taking REAL action, and changing an old habit into new action that will bring us real success in life.

Best Way to Move Forward

The best way to take action is to see and deal with the bigger issues in your life, forgetting for now about the more trivial ones. These trivial ones are most likely triggers from the bigger issues.

You want to remember that being afraid of being alone is a bigger concern than someone standing you up for a date. Though being stood up isn't a fun experience, it is also not a part of the bigger picture.

Think of this process of stepping back from the warmth in front of you to see the blazing fire that's causing the warmth. Always ask yourself what the bigger issue might be, as working on that allows the smaller issues to resolve themselves.

Finding out why you're afraid of being lonely will help you to not be affected by someone standing you up, for example.

The most effective way to use the law of action is to know where you want to be and then look at all the paths you can take to get there. With a clear picture of where you truly want to be in your mind, you will instantly feel a burden lifted. See all the paths you can get to this goal as you do not want to limit options of manifesting. View all these paths you can take to get to the conclusion, FEEL which one makes you happier, passionate, or excited in your entire Being. Start taking action to that path. (Know that this path could change once you have taken action.)

Your action needs to be simple, clear, and flexible in order for this to be effective in taking the right action that will change your life. Even a simple start will get you going towards where you want to be in your life. The most important thing here in taking action is that you stay positive in your life. Keeping your mind open and positive will assist in making the actions simple and easy. This shift of perspective will open doors, enabling you to see and be aware of new and innovative ideas that will open new opportunities to you.

Don't Slow Down the Progress

If there is any place in your life at all that you are having a negative mindset, this will cause frustration and possibly slow down or stop your progress toward whatever you want to manifest. The law of action works when you work toward achieving your dreams. Most people wait until they are in a very negative or uncomfortable situation before they choose to work on the law of action. Remember, it is about making changes in the way you walk your life everyday in **all** situations.

It is much like when people diet. They follow a plan, just for the immediate goal of losing weight, after they do; they go back to the way they ate before the diet. On the other hand, if one is passionate about being healthy and the fringe benefit is perfect weight, then they are more likely to make a lifestyle change permanent. It becomes a way of life everyday to eat better and healthier. The law of action is applied here. In all other life goal dreams, it requires the same passion that it is making a life change in how you perceive your days and what you choose to think and feel and take action on it. With this passion, taking action in this way becomes a way of life.

Learning the law of action towards a dream is to let go and trust. Learning the law of action will allow you to live your life comfortably and continue with your journey to achieve your dreams. Using the law of action and learning to live it moves you away from the problems that used to lead to crisis.

Fear is the one thing that stops us from action and action is all you need to get where it is you want to be. Once you figure out what it is you want, taking action and never giving up will get you there. It will also get you there faster. It is fear and laziness that keep one from truly learning, understanding, and living the law of action.

You may have tried living the law of action and say it does not work. Look at other places in your life you may be carrying or broadcasting low frequencies. That particular area may not have anything to do with what you want to manifest, but if you are broadcasting any low frequencies in any area of your life, it will just return and manifest in other areas of your life, point is low frequency is returning to you. Energy/frequency has no judgment, it just is.

Since frequency is just energy, it does not take on low or high vibration until we give it action which we do from our thoughts. That thought is what determines the low or high vibration. Then it acts as a magnet and it attracts the same vibration. Consider how many times we think positive about what we want to manifest in life, but other low thoughts about other aspects of our lives put out a frequency that is lower. It is really about changing your perception about everything in life and how you view and think of it.

Most times these kinds of thoughts have become habits and we no longer realize we are having them. Becoming conscious again in our lives and paying attention to all we think, say, or do minute-to-minute will amaze you. You begin to realize how much you think or say that you have become unconscious of. So, let's get conscious again.

Law Three Exercises

Exercise One
List all the areas of your life that are not how you would like it to be.

Exercise Two
List all the areas you are aware of that you broadcast or receive low frequencies.

<u>Exercise Three</u>

Now look at ways you can make changes to both of these areas in your life and list them as ACTION steps.

You want to work on these now, later we will add to write a vision of a dream you want to manifest. First we must build a good foundation with our self on taking action in changing the way we are walking daily now.

THE LAW OF CORRESPONDENCE

This universal law states that the principles or laws of physics that explain the physical world-energy, light, vibration, and motion have their corresponding principles in the etheric or universe. As above, so below.

The law of correspondence helps us understand why we act how we do in the world. The world around you is just a reflection of what is going on within your mind or what we call our inner world. What you are thinking becomes your dominant pattern and this will have to show up somewhere.

This law is why and how we show up in the world. The world you create is nothing more than the reflection of your thoughts within your mind or inner world in everyday. For example, if you go through your life, thinking that everyone wants to hurt you, you will see examples of hurtful people all around you.

But if you look at the world as being filled with teachers and with those who can help you, that's also what you will find. The idea of creating your own reality is the key here.

Nothing can happen to or for you unless it conforms from something inside you.

Example: I had a client who I told to visualize their goal and they said they didn't want to, as they thought their thoughts would limit it. In actuality, that is what she IS manifesting; her inner thought that is she will limit it.

Change from the Inside

Like all change, it is made from within first. To improve your life, you must first make a change within yourself. To do this, you will want to change and redesign your thoughts. Your thoughts will change for the better when you change your perception of your beliefs.

Your beliefs are never set in stone. No matter how long you've had an idea or a thought, you don't have to continue to have it. You can change anything you want about yourself, and you don't have to wait one more minute.

Your perception of your beliefs is something that you also want to address. If you feel badly about your beliefs or you question your own right to believe in certain things, this creates chaos in your mind and heart. Instead, think about what you believe, deep down in your gut.

No matter what your beliefs are, when you are confident in them, the world around you responds. Think positively and your world will create positive results.

You are the one that needs to create your beliefs, however. Turning to others for help does not inform who you are. Others can only give you options that you can consider. You want to be the one that decides whether those beliefs work for you.

Plus, when you give over the power of creating your beliefs to another person, you also give over responsibility for creating your own life.

You must be responsible in creating within yourself the equivalent of what you want to experience on the outside. Nothing in life can be manifested, achieved, or created until it is brought to life within your own mind.

The universe is a mirror and just as we focus on something then manifest it in our lives; we then seem to notice more of that around us.

Example

You never think of a certain type of car, you think what qualities in a car you want and manifest it and it comes in a certain make and model. Now, after the fact the mirror also works in this way. Now you are noticing the same kind of car you bought everywhere you go. You attracted that type of car because it fit your qualifications, but now that you have it, they are popping up everywhere – like magic. Not quite. They always were there, but your focus shifted to the one you have and now you are noticing them all over.

The law of correspondence sounds much like the law of attraction, but it is an aspect of that law. All the laws fit and merge together. So, an example of the law of correspondence asks you to review beliefs and perceptions. If you have outgrown a belief or what to change one, you can, but awareness of what they are is just as important.

Example

I told a friend/client that the way I know I have received an answer from the universe is that it occurs three times. I ask for it three times going with my belief: "three times and it is so". She told me after I had told her that, it started happening to her too and she had a new tool. Many of these signs and tools are unconscious and you want to be more conscious of them. For instance, I did not know that was my signal when I was young and growing up. My mother was superstitious and she always said, "Oh my three times and it is so." Everything happened in threes for her. I heard this is the background and never knew I bought it as my belief. When I was older, I commented how weird it was everything came to me three times. It was then that one of teachers pointed out I must have bought it as a belief, but unconsciously.

For the law of correspondence, we want to identify the ones we have unconsciously so we can become a conscious participant in our attractions and how they come to us. Not just what we reflect to us from our thoughts but also understanding how (why) they come to us the way they do. What we are doing here is learning what our unconscious beliefs are and what our language is. Energy when it returns to us speaks to us in our own language, which is matching or mirroring our belief systems, conscious or unconscious. If there are unconscious beliefs, then we would no longer know what those are, right? Taking notice of little things in your life like the 'three and it is so' will assist you in finding many of them and becoming aware of them.

This way we can be present with this law and we can change any of the ones we do not want to occur the way they are in our present time.

You are the Sum

Everything and everyone is a reflection of us, but I want you to focus on just 5 people you are particularly close to in your personal life. If you hang out a lot, then these 5 people are a strong reflection of something you have inside of you. It doesn't mean you act it out, but they reflect something you feel or think inside. Even great qualities we have inside, but you may not have tapped into yet, are a reflection from the ones around us.

Make sure you pay attention to all aspects of your life. Your attitude, health, emotions, wealth, and passions because all parts are being reflected.

When you understand that you are the maker of everything that happens to you, you will understand that your thoughts, behaviors, and actions all determine what your life is like. You can no longer pass the blame for anything that happens in your life. Remember this will include past life thoughts and beliefs too.

We are using blame when we say; if only...

- You would change
- You were more supportive of me
- You quit picking on me
- You love me
- I had more money
- I had more time

Or things like; these things are happening because...

- Of the person I am with
- I have kids and responsibilities
- I am under attack (energy or Being)
- I hate my job

You must understand where these occurrences come from. For example, if you believe it is because of a mate or job that your life is uncomfortable, look inside where you manifested it. First what is it about those that reflect a part of you within, acted out or not? Also, what choices have you made within that has you still in this situation? What beliefs are you holding onto? Is your belief that, "I have to work hard or take any job to be abundant," or, "I am with this person because of convenience or income." Listen to what your soul tells you.

If you REALLY look and understand the law of correspondence, you will become excited, as this law opens a new door to freedom. It will show you what you have worked on and what you consciously wanted to experience. It will also show you parts within that were hidden even from you that you now can consciously choose to transmute and make new. Not just because you will attract what you want, but because you have healed a part within and this is why you are attracting it.

In conclusion, nothing in this world controls us but our thoughts. To take control of your thinking and not blocking it, but transmuting it, you take control of your life. This law also shows us we control HOW we see the world around us. It will awaken many a-ha moments, no matter how far along you are in self-awareness.

When I speak of taking control of thoughts, I actually mean to stop, and choose your thoughts. You can transmute old and negative thought patterns by choosing to change how you perceive something and then choose a different way to think of it.

Let's look at how all the laws so far integrate:

Lower frequencies make us feel separate from our Oneness. Thoughts are frequencies and by being conscious of frequencies, transmuting them, and seeing which ones we have within that are still low frequencies, this knowledge assists us in becoming ONE as we transmute undesired energies. In doing so, we remove the separation layer-by-layer. After understanding this, take action in your life. Action can be as simple as changing your thoughts and reactions we have in life.

Law Four Exercises

Exercise One
Sit and reflect on beliefs you have now that are very apparent to you and jot them down.

Then ask yourself are there any of them you want to change.

Ask are there any beliefs of which you were not aware, like you have to work hard to get far; everything happens in the 11th hour, if I got this_____, it would be a miracle. Many times, the beliefs are not negative but if we think we need a miracle for something, then that is what it will take.

Are there any of these beliefs you would like to change?

Exercise Two

List 5 people you are close to or hang out with regularly. List mirrored qualities you are aware of in them when they are with you.

Now list all the things they do that might irritate or frustrate you. Look within for thoughts or feelings you have that you may have not been aware of that match these.

Now list all the things you love about them and all their qualities and do the same as above for this one too.

Exercise Three

List any places in your life that are not where you would like them to be: attitude, health, relationships, friends, etc.

Then find what this knowledge reflects to you. Think about that which you own within.

Write how you would like your reflection to be. What thoughts or actions would you choose to change to support the way you want things to be?

Now take action.

THE LAW OF CAUSE AND EFFECT

The law cause and effect is saying whatever energy you put out into the world is the energy that will come back to you. This universal law states that nothing happens by chance or outside the universal laws. Every action has a reaction or consequence and we "reap what we have sown."

Have you ever noticed days that seem to be so messed up everything seems to be going wrong? You stub your toe, hit your head, are late for an appointment, and you say to yourself, "This is the worst day possible!" This is the law working.

What Can You Do?

With this law, you have total control at what effects come into your life. Our thoughts bring about actions and these actions bring about the effects we see in our lives.

I'm not saying that a mind full of all loving thoughts will mean your life will be **only** of love, but you will find that life does go a lot smoother when you focus on the positive things.

I find that instead of finding the reason why something is going wrong in your life, it's more effective to find the goodness within your life and you'll be a thousand times happier.

If you are open to what you are putting into the universe, you will find that you do put a much better energy out, bringing in effects that are more full of joy.

These are some steps you can take when your day seems to be out of alignment.

Step One: As soon as you feel your day is out of alignment, stop, get in neutral, get in present moment and take notice what is going on.

Step Two: Do not judge anything about it, just begin to notice it.

Step Three: Ask yourself, "What thought did I have to start this process?"

Step Four: Ask what you can do to accept what is going on and begin to direct it into a better energy?

Step Five: Think what part(s) of your life is/are going well and place all your energy into that energy. Focus on this energy.

Step Six: Find the place where you were the cause and change it so that the effect changes.

Step Seven: Now that you found the cause and effect, celebrate your ability to affect your world.

These steps can assist you daily with in-the-moment manifestations. The fact is although many things we are now experiencing in our life were from a past choice; we are still living the experience out.

Many think if they made a poor choice now, they have to deal with the fallout. To a degree this is true, but many less joyful choices we have made are really just choices showing us where our thinking is still in life and about life. If we feel we are always victimized, we will always make less joyful choices that put us in situations of being the victim. All of this is an outer reflection of what is believe inside. They are all lessons. You can also learn to see the lesson and once you do make a new and more positive choice.

If your life has felt as if it has had many bad days, weeks, years and months now, then this is just saying you have not learned the lesson yet. When you truly do not want this experience anymore, you can use the steps just used for daily and apply them to longer time periods.

Example

I keep getting in dysfunctional relationships.

Look back to the first one, look at your upbringing, and look at what made you make the choice to be with each person. Have you changed? Do you love yourself more now and realize you deserve better in life? Instead of thinking on how much you do not like your life, transmute those thoughts and start saying to yourself: *I deserve better now and I am now walking towards a more joyful life.* This alone will start opening opportunities for you to make new choices to walk towards a new life, even if those first steps are walking out of an old life first.

Look at any long-term experiences that have been less joyful in your life. Then use the tools in the earlier chapter on changing your perception of them. Reword those stories so you can transmute them and heal inside.

Many have a belief you cannot change Karma, cause, and effect, yet every time you make a new and more joyful choice, you already have. Since you create your Karma, you only need to be conscious of that and make new choices. The biggest thing about Karma is that it's about learning your lessons.

Law Five Exercises

Exercise One

Look at places in your life where things feel wrong, or at places where things are not going the way you want them to. Then look further back to what thought or decision was the cause of the now effect that you are living now.

Exercise Two

After examining your life, what choices can you make today to start and change the effects to come?

UNIVERSAL LAW SIX

THE LAW OF COMPENSATION

This universal law of compensation is the law of cause and effect, applied to the blessings and abundance we receive. The sixth law is the manifested results of our deeds that are given to us in the forms of gifts, money, inheritances, friendships, and blessings.

This law is firm and there is no flexibility in the rules. The law is clear and straight forward, as it means we cannot have successes without also having failures or hardships. Compensation in more clear terms is, "For everything you have missed, you have gained something else and for everything you gain, you have lost something else."

For anything and everything gained, there must be a loss. A simple example would be in order to have a fire to stay warm; we use the wood, which means we replace the wood for the fire and warmth. Now we cook food on the fire, we replace the heat from the fire with the food we cook. We then lose the food to bring nourishment to our bodies. This continues until the energy is so small we move on. Loss is not meant in the human concept of it being a negative thing. One thing always balances the other.

The Law of Nature

Some would call this the law of nature, which brings balance and harmony to the world. Many Masters have contemplated nature for this very reason. In the New Age practice, we might at first believe the only purpose of meditating in nature is to enjoy the beauty, the calm, and the serenity found in nature. Many students of esoteric teachers are guided to meditate with and in nature in order to understand this law. For the real reason we are guided to meditate with nature is to learn about balance among many other great lessons.

Examples include:

a) Insects can destroy forests at times, but in other cases without insects to eat certain algae or other forms of things that would harm the environment, our animals would die off.

b) A tree is hit by lightning and dies off, and we might find this sad, as it means the loss of a tree. But for anything lost, there is a gain. This tree will rot and go back to the Mother Earth and will create wonderfully rich compost that will make new plants grow and thrive where it has rotted.

In order to understand and use this law, we must realize that whatever we place in the world has to be replaced. This is the law of compensation at work.

How Does This Work in Our Lives?

Look at it this way: if you plant seeds of love, you will be loved, and if you plant acts of kindness then others will treat you kindly. If you emanate anger you will sow hostility.

This gives new meaning to the quote, "No man can help another without helping themselves."

With this said, many would ask: how then is this law working in my life when I have put nothing but good and love into the world, yet I have sown hardships or experience a lack in abundance?

The law of compensation once again is, "For every loss is a gain, for every gain is a loss."

When the energies were denser on this planet it took a long time for cause and effect to return to one person, sometimes another lifetime all together. What you put out when you were twelve years old took until you were twenty-three years old to return in the balance of that energy. With the planet vibrations being so high and accelerated now, this is not the case and we can have a return in a short amount of time. As the energies accelerated, you also brought any effects to a cause in faster even from other lives.

Maybe in one year you had the return balance of energy that occurred many lifetimes ago. What you emanate out now though has almost instant return. This does not erase the return of the other lifetimes for balance. If you have been working on putting out good, love, etc. for the last two or three years, but found many hardships happening, these could be a return of energy from other times. The good news is the return of many lifetimes will process and move quicker than they would have before, so the worst may already be over.

We must remember to put the two meanings together. Someone may be rich in this life but unhappy, where another may be poor but very happy. It still is the effect of a cause, whether it was this lifetime or not. Or you may have a rich corporate leader but he is so bogged down with work he never finds time to enjoy it and live and have time off. Again this could be in another life he was poor and in this life to have the balance he is rich, but if his unhappiness stems from a different cause from other lives, they might want to balance out in this life.

Because of the energies returning to us at an accelerated rate today, we can also move much of our karma more quickly. So to become in balance, we can process more quickly as well.

The Law of Compensation Brings Change

For those who want to change their lives using the law of compensation, does it mean that they must go through pain of loss to gain a different life?

Only each individual going through the change can answer that. We realize that there is no gain without loss, in understanding this law, you can instead ask yourself, "What am I willing to give up?" You can grow with the knowledge that something must go to be replaced with the gain.

The concepts of this law are addressed in other teachings, such as the law of attraction, but it is often not explained as a law of the universe on its own. We don't hear about it and yet we understand that there IS the law of compensation. How have we heard about this before?

a) One way is we are told to clean out our clutter, give things away, or take them to a donation service. Make space to bring in something more.

b) If you want a relationship, make space in your living quarters as if you are bringing it in.

These are not acts under the law of attraction as we are taught. They are basics of the law of compensation.

If you wanted to start a successful business, you may say you are willing to give up time for the energy of success. It is not a loss of time; it is balancing the scales, taking something out to gain something in.

If you are going through times of struggle, change how you look at that. Instead of looking at it as negative, when we have challenges or setbacks in our growth, we can know they are blessings waiting to be discovered because of our experience. If we understand the law, we know any difficult times or struggles **MUST** be replaced with times of blessings and success.

Understanding the law will also assist you in moving towards those blessings and successes more quickly and more joyously. You can begin by asking, "What is the lesson in my difficulties that I want to know and learn?" The answer may be as simple as law of compensation and you are currently doing nothing in this moment or time to make this occur. Many times, we drive ourselves batty looking for what we have done or blaming ourselves for difficulties in the moment. It is good to look and see if we have created this in our NOW by how we are thinking and living, but do not forget to also ask, is this law of compensation at work here?

If you are going to move into a place of great success, it may be that you are balancing it now by putting in time, work, and maybe some discomfort, but that will be replaced with joy, more time, and successes.

Law Six Exercises

Exercise One

In order for you to fully understand this law, look back in your life at any times of struggle. After you look back, remember what it was like when that time was over.

What greatness or blessings came into your life after that?

Exercise Two

Look at your life today and see if any of it feels like a struggle. If so, look at it differently and see what might be replaced up the road for this struggle. The replacement will be based on other laws, such as where your thinking and heart is. Less joyful or more joyful? Change your perception now.

Exercise Three
If all is good in your life right now, look back at what you might have gone through that for which you are now reaping the rewards.

Exercise Four
Remember that with the acceleration on the planet even past life karma is processing faster, so apply the accelerated ascension energies to this law for today. Know that the energy you put in now will pay off more quickly.

Exercise Five
If you cannot see any correlation with certain struggles in this lifetime with anything you went through in this life, then meditate and journey to the time when the cause occurred, and what the effects are now.

Many times just knowing what happened in the past and the lessons that may be involved will move the energy much quicker in your present time. If you are not someone who knows how to journey on your own, find someone who takes others on a journey to past lives.

Exercise Six
For future manifestations to be more joyful state:

Now I am giving _____, to be replaced with this _____.

Example: I am giving up excess weight to be replaced with good health.

Once we understand the law, we can choose how to balance that cause and effect and we can walk through our lives more joyfully.

THE LAW OF ATTRACTION

Others Call It "The Secret" But It Is No Secret And Never Was!

The law of attraction is a popular one – and one that gets a lot of discussion. This law demonstrates how we create and manifest the things, events, people, and experiences in our life. *Like attracts like.* <u>Thought is energy.</u> This law is how we experience physical and mental manifestations. The thoughts (energy), feelings (energy), words (energy), and actions (energy) all work together to manifest in our lives, they lead us in the direction we choose in life.

Everything in the world is energy. You are energy, your computer is energy, your phone is energy, the trees are energy, etc. At the core of everything is energy. As we are all made of molecules, we are all the same energy.

As Carl Sagan said, "We are all stardust." And when you think about it this way, you can see how the law of attraction is something that is, not something that you need to believe.

Think of each one of the above, thought, feeling, words, and actions as individual frequencies. It is the combination of these frequencies that assist us in manifesting. This is why just having positive thoughts will NOT manifest what you want. It requires all of the frequencies combined to have the correct recipe for what you want to manifest.

Once we understand this law in its entirety, we understand we have control over our own reality. We can begin to direct our lives in a way we want consciously. The law of attraction comes from all thought, emotion, and action, whether it is conscious or unconscious. This may have been the only 'secret' about the law to most people. Many times, people feel they are having conscious thoughts and feelings that are positive, yet have had a negative experience and wonder why. This situation is because the law also works with unconscious thoughts and feelings. The best way to truly manifest the life you want is to work on the unconscious thoughts and feelings and transmute those that do not fit our higher good.

The law of attraction is saying:

- You get what you ask for.
- You get what you think about.
- Your thoughts determine your experience(s).
- Your emotions and feelings give your life direction.

Our thoughts are energy and attract like energy to them. Our feelings are what fuels the thoughts and direct the experiences. If we want to have conscious participation in our manifesting, we must learn and live these four steps:

1. Know what you truly desire and ask the Universe (god, goddess, angels, higher self) for it.

2. Keep your focus on what you truly desire throughout your day.

3. Use your feelings as the catalyst to manifest your desires by acting as if your desire is already here (FEEL your desire is

already here, such as feeling emotions of love, celebrating the success, gratitude, etc.)

4. Be open and know you are deserving of receiving it and do not limit how it may manifest in your life.

With the law of attraction, it is so important to work on any unconscious thoughts or feelings you have about lack, being undeserving, and fears of failure, lack of trust or faith and such. If these are unconscious thoughts stuck in the subconscious, then these will be emanating the polarity of your conscious thoughts and sabotage your manifestations of what you truly desire.

The mirror also works on attracting our subconscious thoughts or polarity beliefs. If I say, "I am abundant" three times, every hour and then when my friends ask if I would like to go to a movie, I say (with emotion happening inside of me), "I can't. I am really broke." I have just put that out into the world and it will attract that situation back to me, creating more scarcity in my finances.

Another way we sabotage what we attract is with fear. Chanting a mantra every day that we are in a relationship and happy doesn't help when inside we have a lot of fear about falling in love again. This disparity will repel a relationship from coming into our lives. So we attract more of being alone.

Another method of sabotage is to not feeling worthy or not conceiving that we really can have what we want to attract in our life. Because of this, it is important to understand and become aware of our fears and subconscious thoughts so we are attracting in a healthy way what we truly want.

Your thoughts might begin to work against you.

You can work with these through meditations or using my book or workbook (Awaken the Secret Within, Keys to Joyful Living) with daily exercises and worksheets to find these unconscious thoughts and feelings. Also, since like attracts like, whatever you are experiencing in life is a mirror. If you have struggle or discomfort then it is showing you what your unconscious thoughts and feeling are. They HAVE manifested and can be used as a tool to see what areas you want to work on in your life.

On the fourth step, after feeling deserving and being open to receiving, you then want to be open and unlimited in how your experience may come to you. Many times it will come in ways you could never dream of.

Example

I was always told I would be in the media and go global with my ideas. I could not imagine how I would do that especially because at the time I was a single mom of 5 children. How was this possible?

Instead of thinking this was impossible; I just held the knowing if it was of Divine order it would happen. I lived my life knowing my angels and guides would bring it to me. One day, I gave a soul reading to a man who really connected with me. Time had gone by and without my knowing, he felt I had saved his life with one of my readings, though I had no conscious knowledge of this during the reading.

He later gave me a public broadcast show and a producer. He then paid all my travel expenses to tape the show, and also paid the travel expenses of my guests on the show every month. I would have never thought of it to come to me in this way. It was more of my trust and faith that my guides always bring me to what I want and I am always provided for. At this time, I was still working on the deserving part, but because I believed strongly and without doubt if it was my soul purpose, I manifested this possibility and the outcome.

It was the FEELINGS of that trust that fueled the direction of the outcome.

There are many ways to work with the law of attraction. Here is just one list that can begin to assist the process.

1. FEEL/Passion – Find within what is truly a strong desire or passion of what you want in life.

2. Clarity – Become clear on what it is you want and also what you already have that you wanted.

3. Ask - Ask for what you want from the universe, your higher self, God, etc.

4. Believe – You must truly believe you deserve it, you want it, and that what you want is possible.

5. Explore/Discover – Look at your life right now and the abundance you have now. Picture your ideal life and then look for daily examples that match it.

6. Celebrate – Celebrate as if your dream is here now and remember to FEEL gratitude NOW, not when it gets here. Know it is here already because all realities exist at once.

7. Trust/Faith – Feel your trust and faith daily, minute to minute until it becomes a part of you.

If you master even two of these seven methods above, you will realize you are strong and that you are already a manifester of your life. You will gain confidence that can make this law work every day.

Law Seven Exercises

Exercise 1
Meditate and ask what thoughts or feelings you have that are unconscious. Ask your higher self or guides to bring them to your conscious mind so you can work on them.

Exercise 2

If you feel you are still unclear on your subconscious thoughts, then make note of what is uncomfortable in your life or what negative feeling(s) you have now. Meditate and ask to see what core issues are attached to them. You can use books to look up the issue for more insight such as "Heal Your Body," by Louise Hay.

Exercise 3

Write a clear statement of what you truly want in your life.

Exercise 4

Write down what you are passionate about in your life.

Exercise 5

Go through each of the seven steps until you FEEL each one of them as a part of you, own them in relation to the dream you have or the experience you want to attract in your life.

THE LAW OF TRANSMUTATION OF ENERGY

This law simply means that energy is always in movement, and that all energy eventually moves into physical form. Energy is perpetually present. As we have covered before, this will include our thoughts and our pictures in our heads, for these are energy too. Because we have thoughts constantly, according to this law, they will eventually manifest into physical form.

No matter what your thoughts or pictures are, they will, at some time, manifest into the physical plane. If your thoughts are fear, worry, or depression, that is what will manifest. If your thoughts and pictures are of joy, happiness, and security then that must also manifest.

Have you ever heard someone say, "I cannot stick up for myself at work. If I do, I will get fired." Then one day they have had enough of the stress and have let it build up and they release it one day at work and then they get fired. Then you hear that person say, "See? I knew that would happen."

The reason this really happened is because that person thought it enough times that they gave it energy and then that had to be the outcome, according to this law. The thought had occurred so many times that it became energy in motion and it manifested into a reality. If you have thoughts like this on a regular basis, it builds a lot of energy behind it and becomes like an avalanche. If you thought about anything for long enough in your life, it becomes energy in motion that is difficult to stop or transmute. It would be like holding your hands up in the air and trying to push an avalanche back up a mountain.

A more everyday occurrence with people: You may be going through a time of only making ends meet financially, so your thoughts become of fear, worry, and lack. The more you have those thoughts, the more that being in lack will manifest and persist in your life.

Because you believed in it and created persistent thoughts about it.

The Law of Transmutation of Energy

This law makes itself present for everyone on the planet. Each person's life will show them exactly where their thoughts and pictures have been. A successful person in life will bring success to their life, which means their thoughts and pictures have been focused on being successful. A person who always thinks in failure will manifest failure in their life.

A successful person would see a great home or car and look at it and say with confidence and assurance, "I will have that." They feel and know inside they will. Someone who is manifesting failure will look at the same thing and think, "I would like to have that someday, but it probably will never happen."

Being conscious of the law of perpetual transmutation can work in your favor by encouraging you to be more aware of what your thoughts and pictures are. If things are in a place right now that you're not happy with in your life, you can change this by transmuting your thoughts and pictures, which will then transmute your energy. Ask yourself right now:

- What are your daily thoughts?
- What do you worry about?

- What fears are you thinking about?
- What are you putting energy to in your life?

Pay attention to your thoughts and how your mind and body is feeling when you have them. This is important, as your body will let you know how you feel about your thoughts, whether they are negative or positive. Your body will tell you by tense shoulders, neck, tightness in your throat, or you may feel a racing or tenses in a chakra area.

If you do not like your thoughts, choose consciously to change them. Even if your body still reacts in the same way it did before, noticing this feeling and how it does change the more you begin to replace your negative thoughts will show you your thoughts have shifted to a new energy.

Example

Let's say you become aware that you always say in your mind, "I will never have true love." When you have this thought, your body feels heavy or drained and you feel sad in your heart. You decide to consciously change this thought to, "I will have true love in my life." But your body may still feel heavy and drained and your heart may still be sad. This feeling is a sign you have NOT truly changed your thought, you are just saying words, but your thought is still supporting the old thought.

You want to keep saying you will have love until you feel your body shift in how it reacts and then you will know you have actually broken the old thought pattern.

Transmuting Energy

If you find your thoughts manifest what you do not want in your life, immediately add another higher thought at the time of that recognition. Since energy is always moving, always flowing, you can immediately change the energy of that thought – you can transmute the energy.

Pay attention after transmuting your thoughts (energy) and watch for the new manifestation they take in your life. Remember, energy is just energy until we label it, and once we do we have given it a direction to manifest.

This is why we also want to release old energy meaning old pictures and old thoughts. As we release old energy patterns, this makes room to bring in new forms of energy. As this new energy comes in, we shape and form what that energy will look like in the physical existence, based on our thoughts and pictures. We can shape that energy by labeling and FEELING it to be true, and only then can it manifest what we truly desire.

So Why Do I Feel It Isn't Working?

Many people confuse the eighth law, law of transmutation of energy with the law of attraction. They feel if they just make a vision board of what they want, start thinking positive, or if they follow the law of action and just take steps and meet the right contacts, they will manifest what they want in their life. This is a good place to start, but it's not the end of the process.

You can find two people in life that have the same talents, the same contacts, and the same opportunities on their paths, but one will become extremely successful and the other may have minimal success. Why does this happen?

Where is the Right Place to Start?

Many start by changing their thoughts. That is good, but if you do not truly understand and are not conscious of what you are doing, it will take longer to manifest. In some cases, you will continue to sabotage yourself.

It is not just about being aware that you change your thoughts. It IS about knowing and understanding. What does that mean? It means to become aware that you are working with energy and you want to know you are working with energy. When you have a thought, be AWARE you are playing with energy and you are about to move it out into the world. Be AWARE that it is energy and, with conscious intent, you are about to transmute that energy.

Energy will manifest into physical form, regardless of you being aware that it is. When you consciously participate in what you are putting out in the world to manifest, you can have a more joyful and successful path. If you choose to ignore this and live unconsciously, the results are still that you are manifesting into physical what your unconscious thoughts are but your perception is that you are experiencing these incidents in your life randomly.

Many who are manifesting unconsciously also feel things in life are happening TO them. Being conscious of this law also accelerates your growth and experiences you choose to have in life.

I am Doing All of This and Still Having Experiences I Do Not Want

I have many clients say to me that they are following all of this. They insist they are being conscious and they have worked on a more happy life to be more successful and it still is not happening. In most of these cases, they are in a marriage, partnership, or have children and other family members who are also in their lives and also manifesting their own energy thoughts. Many times we have made a soul agreement to play scenarios out with others for lessons and so we are also affected by what they are manifesting, especially if we live with them. This might happen to you too.

Ask yourself what your lesson is with these people and with these shared experiences. Then apply this law to manifest the experience that you learn the lesson and in a more joyful manner.

In many of the cases I have described above, the lesson is as simple as wanting to let go of the relationship or relationships. We choose what we want to experience so if we are engaging with family, friends or mates that are following a path of resistance and heavy lower vibrational lives, we still have the choice to participate in that life or not. If a person truly wants to manifest happiness in life and this is just not occurring with the people in their life, then the lesson could be to just let go. To go and manifest new people in their lives that reflect what they want in life may be the only option. If they do not, then on some level they may not truly want happiness. As stated earlier, we want to release old energies to create space for new energies to come into our lives.

No matter how you look at it, you are still manifesting your thoughts and pictures that have made your life what it is now.

Meditate on a regular basis and be conscious of the energy and what energy you are sending out. If you do not like it, transmute it. This is the way the law was always intended to be used.

Law Eight Exercises

Exercise 1
Take a thought you no longer want. Sit and meditate with it and FEEL it, see it, sense what that energy labeled as your thought feels like, etc. See it and know it as its energy form.

Exercise 2
Take a new and positive thought and do the same as above.

Exercise 3
Now take the first thought (negative or heavy) and as you are seeing and feeling it, change it to something else in your meditation. How does that feel or look?

Exercise 4
Practice daily being aware in the moment you are having a thought with conscious intent to manifest what you want.

Exercise 5

Ask and explore within yourself, are you choosing to keep relationships with anyone that do not reflect the higher vibrational life you want?

Exercise 6

If you are, look for fears, worries, or any old program blocks that you still have within that is still manifesting this unhappiness in life or discomfort.

Exercise 7

Meditate, meditate, and then meditate, and start seeing all as energy.

THE LAW OF RELATIVITY

This universal law states that each person will receive a series of events (tests/initiations) for the purpose of strengthening the Light Within. When we see these tests as lessons for growth, we stay connected to our hearts and we grow and become stronger from these lessons. This education teaches us to compare our lessons to others' lessons in order to put everything in its proper perspective. No matter how challenging our lessons are, others around us may be experiencing more difficult lessons in life.

The eighth law concerns how we view an object, incident, or event – our interpretation. Nothing is bad or good until we interpret it to be so. When you witness an object, incident, or an experience in life, it will not take on energy until you interpret it. This interpretation will be based on your past experiences.

You will look at a situation and then compare it to something that is negative or positive based on past. When you observe a situation and compare it to something **more** difficult, than the situation at hand starts to look better. This can also happen in the opposite where looking at a situation and then compare to something that feels and looks better, then the situation at hand will look worse.

The key here is nothing is good or bad until you relate it to something else.

With this law, we find that all things are relative to each other. All of the laws are related to each other and interconnect and are really all one. There is no bad or good, right or wrong, until we compare it to something else.

When the Law of Relativity is Used Properly

Understanding this law completely will assist you in flowing through life effortlessly. One example of this law in motion is if you see someone and decide they do something better than you, then you have to also see and know that you do things that are better than others. More commonly, you interpret that someone has mastered something you cannot do yourself, and you interpret that this makes you look bad at it. In doing this, you are looking at the surface level, and in this case the law is working against you.

If instead you look at the same situation and see someone has mastered something and focus on the things in life you have mastered and see it in this way, you will build your own self esteem. You will see how special you are and you will be consciously aware of the best that you can be. If you interpret this law of relativity as a lesson which appears to be a problem, then these are the two possible reactions you will get:

- The victim reaction
- The growth reaction

If you use the law of relativity which is to compare things that are going on around you, and if you respond as a victim such as:

- "Why me?"
- "This stuff always happens to me"
- "I am always shorter, slower, underpaid"

Then you have chosen to slow down your spiritual growth.

On the other hand if you choose to use the law of relativity as seeing situations in your life as a starting point in life, meaning you choose to interpret it from a more positive place such as:

- "I may not be where you are, but I am still learning."
- "I may be slow but I will get faster."
- "This law has shown me I am not where I want to be, yet when I do get there, I will have grown spiritually."

If you choose to use the law of relativity in this way, then this law will guide you with ease. You will be conscious that you have a choice. This law shows you comparisons that will make you aware that things in life are in constant motion, change, and you can choose to move your journey quickly and more productively.

Each one of us is on a journey and the lessons will be unique to our own lives and soul path. The law suggests we look at comparisons, but it is spiritual growth when we see the comparisons as lessons and not good or bad or more or less. It is about the interpretations of the comparisons. Make sure it is the eyes of interpretation you are looking through and not the eyes of judgment.

Ask the Right Questions

When met with the law of comparison, ask the questions that assist in your growth such as, "What am I to learn from this?" and "How will this assist me to further my spiritual growth?" In doing this the comparison is not a negative interpretation of anyone else.

If you approach the law in this way, then each lesson you meet in your life will give you what you want on this journey towards healing, growth, and the evolution of your soul. It will assist you in becoming enlightened on your journey.

The biggest lesson here is to be conscious that choices are made from our heart and not from your ego. Ego would lead to judgment. Begin to look at every situation as relative, and it is your interpretation of it that assists you to grow or to be victimized by your own self and your judgments.

Examples

Judgment: That person is richer than me and has a better life.

Conscious of the law: That person has mastered abundance and happiness, and I too am learning to embrace that in life.

Judgment: That person is healing and growing spiritually faster than I.

Conscious of the law: By seeing where that person has grown shows me where my own growth will lead.

You may say, why compare at all? In this journey of the human walk we all compare, we must, it is the law. Many say because they are spiritually evolved and healed they no longer compare, but they do, it is just unconscious.

Example: I lived in a house with a large yard, it had a creek behind it and it was wonderful. I could fit three gazebos in it and I had lights everywhere and it was magical. I then moved to a new place and it was a very small yard and had houses behind it instead of a creek. For a long time I was not happy in this yard until I realized I was comparing it to what I had. I then chose to look at this yard with its own uniqueness and started to decorate and put plants in it for the way this yard was. I then found as much joy in it as I did the other.

If we use the law consciously, then we use the law of relativity in the healthy sense, even as we are still comparing. When in the unhealthy sense, we use the law by seeing through the eyes of judgment, not interpretation.

Every day, a thought or two makes a comparison about something.

Be conscious of this law in your daily activities and choose to walk the law with flow and growth.

Law Nine Exercises

Exercise One

Pay attention to your thoughts and pay attention for comparisons. This could be as simple as, "Wow, I like that car, and I wish it were mine." This is a comparison, because the car you want is interpreted in the mind as being better than the one you own.

Exercise Two

Write down larger thoughts that are in the forefront of your mind, such as:
I will be happier when I have a mate, divorce, house, etc.
You are comparing the now to something ahead you think is better.

Exercise Three

Take the answers from # 2 and rewrite your interpretations, such as:
If you wrote I will be happier when I have a mate, you want to write how you can choose to be happy now and all the things in life you have now that make you happy.

Exercise Four

Consciously change in the moment how you see these comparisons as you are having them.

THE LAW OF POLARITY

The universal law of polarity states that everything has an opposite. It is also the law of mental vibration. This law assists us to learn and discover that all things in life contain a solution. In every perceived failure is a success.

What is important to understand with this law is that no matter where you are in your life right now that in each of our lives experiences and how we see them is the possibility and ability to experience the polar opposite. According to this law, our lives have an unlimited amount of possibilities. Because of this, we can travel on our journey in any direction that we choose.

Acceptance and Surrender

This law of polarity helps us to learn the lessons of acceptance and surrender in whatever we are experiencing in our lives. Every experience and circumstance we have in life is happening to give us an active lesson. These lessons assist us and help us understand that everything in our life is working together for our own good. This is the truth no matter how we perceive those events or experiences.

The law of polarity tells us that anything and everything can be split into two different experiences. Each of these experiences holds unlimited possibilities within them. Know this by observing that everything has an opposite.

Example

If we did not know death, we would not appreciate life, if we did not know poverty or financial struggle we would not understand gratefulness of abundance. If we did not experience heartache we would not know heartfelt love to its fullest.

Because we have the gift of free will here on the planet and we have the ability to create our experiences here, then we can choose what part of the polarity we want to experience. If you choose joy, love, and abundance then by transforming your thoughts, feelings, and actions, this is what you will experience. Many times people do not choose these until they have experienced the polarity to the point they no longer want to feel that way in their experiences.

Example

It may take someone having years of drama and chaos in their life before they choose to walk the polarity, which is peace and harmony. Some walk this way more than one lifetime until they learn they have the free will to choose and change their course.

You Always Have a Choice

Our consciousness brings all events that we experience in life in the way that we have chosen to experience it. So, if you do not like the experience you are having then change it by changing what you choose to focus on. Consciously choose first what experience do you want to have? Then change your thoughts and feelings, and take action to create that experience.

When you truly come to an understanding of this truth and reality and embrace that you choose your experiences, you have learned that you are personally responsible for your desired experience, whether you are having it right now or not. Once you truly KNOW this in all fibers of your Being, then you have made a step forward to achieving self mastery.

If your experience now is a life of debt, struggle, lack of love in your life, then just **STOP!** Step back from the situation and look what is actually occurring in your life. You want to stop and realize on some level you have chosen this side of the polarity to learn lessons. Then decide and feel it inside that you now choose to change this experience. Remember, it is not good or bad, it just is. You will learn the lesson completely by choosing to walk the polarity of this situation.

If you want to experience abundance, harmony, and love in your life, KNOW all you have to do is **choose** it. Choosing a different reality consciously and knowing within you chose the polarity to learn from, then it will manifest much quicker than if you attempt to change the experience because of ego-based beliefs.

Example

If you want to attract money or love purely for the reason that you believe it will make you happier in life and you change your thoughts and feelings and take action, you may attract it to you through the law of attraction, but it may take longer to actually manifest this desired outcome. It may also teach you that it did not bring you happiness and that that was ego talking.

If you want the abundance and love because you desire to learn all you can from it to evolve and grow, and to do so is to choose the polarity of lack of love and debt, then this experience will manifest quicker in your life.

The only difference in which of the two opposite experiences occur is which you believe to be true. Your clarity of intent (focus) is what brings a vibration which, when combined with the other laws, brings energies that are harmonious to your belief.

Right/Wrong~ Good/Bad
Are They real?

In order to live and understand the law of polarity, you must apply the law of relativity here. To live the law of polarity, you must understand there is no right and wrong, or good and bad. These items stem from what you choose from the polarities to experience in your life. The chosen polarity is a vibrational energy that you project and because of that you will receive or attract the experiences that resonates with that vibrational energy. If you are labeling one or the other as good or bad or right or wrong, you are adding frequencies that will change the vibration and in doing so change the way you attract the polarity to you and the outcome of the polarity.

Example

If I choose to experience love and abundance and at this current time I am in debt and lack of love, then if I interpret the lack as bad or wrong, then even though I change my thoughts and feelings, I still subconsciously see myself moving from bad to good or from wrong to right. That adds a low vibration frequency to my changing direction and may affect the time line of manifesting the polarity or it may change the way I walk the journey to the love and abundance. I may experience no more heart pain or great debt, but I may then walk a path of no debt but low money, or no heart pain from a bad relationship but first experience loneliness before having love.

If I see myself moving from one polarity to the other, as I move from debt to riches, or lack of love to a life full of love and neither is good or bad, right or wrong, just a different experience, then the vibration stays true to itself and can and will only produce the polarity experience itself. In these two cases, the experience becomes one of riches and abundance of love.

Any other experience would be impossible to bring to life.

Many ask, then why doesn't this happen to more people? Good question. The human mind is complex because we make it that way. We have to walk each of the laws through the layers of consciousness before we can master them. When we do, we have become our own inner Master as all masters before us. See and know you are a Master in training and walk the experiences from who you are at this moment. When you want to change an experience, each time you do, you will master more and more how to get to just polarity, without the right and wrong and bad and good.

The Law of Polarity States that You Have the Right to Experience Life the Way You Choose

The law of polarity has no judgment as to what each of you chooses to experience. It exists for the sole purpose that you can choose what polarity to experience in life. Many wonder how to master these laws and choices. You master them with gaining knowledge of them and by having life experiences with them - consciously.

What You Resist the Most Will Persist

Having acceptance of whatever you are experiencing acts as the polar opposite of resistance and will attract more of your desires. This means that any resistance you have by focusing on the experience and interpreting it bad or good will attract more of what you are resisting.

Acceptance does not mean you want to stay in the experience you are having, it is accepting that that is where you are in the moment. Not labeling it bad or good, right or wrong, it just is where you are right now and you accept it. When you can accept it, you can then decide to change it by choosing to walk the polarity experience of it.

Learn to accept and celebrate the experiences you have already had and the ones you are currently having no matter how they may appear. It is after you do this that you will notice your new choices of the polarity experiences will begin to appear and the other experiences will disappear. Surrender to acceptance of the journey and embrace the entire journey to bring harmony to your life.

Law Ten Exercises

Exercise One
List anything in your life right now that you would like to experience the polarity of.

Exercise Two
Take one of those off the list and in meditation or write a story, write out what the polarity would look like and feel like.

Example: I am insecure and self conscious of my looks
Polarity: I am confident and love myself the way I am

Now write a story about the one that is confident and loves themselves. How do they act, and feel? What are they doing in home life, work life, and playtime? How do they walk each of the laws? Write it in detail.

Exercise Three
Now walk, act, and feel daily the chosen experience of the positive polarity every day until you own it.

Exercise Four
At a later time, do each one on the list.

Exercise Five
Meditate on a Master you like. If you do not know of one, read of one. Look at what they were able to do and walk in their life as a Master, then ask to meet your own Master within. Write about the experience.

Exercise Six
Find where and what you judge as good or bad, right, or wrong and work on acceptance by perceiving it differently.

THE LAW OF RHYTHM

The law of rhythm says there is a rhythm that occurs all of the time. The rhythm is like the tide that goes in and out, or like the way the sun rises and sets.

Everything that manifests in life can be measured in motion. There is always action and reaction; an advance and a retreat; a rising and sinking. Many think this is just the law of polarity, but it is things of polarity and not polarity that are a motion of rhythm as ebb and flow. This law also occurs in the seasons, in life and death of all things. Like the saying, "What goes around, comes around."

You Can Make Use of The Law OR Let It Use You

Before I fully understood this law, I used to go from one extreme to the other. Now going from one side to the other is like a pendulum and that is a rhythm, if you consciously walk it that way. But when you swing from one to the other, not riding the momentum of the pendulum, then you are living the law by letting it use you. If you ride the pendulum with consciousness of the rhythm that is occurring, then you are making use of the law.

To have rhythm, we know if there is love, then there is lack of love. If swinging from one extreme to the other we will have love in intensity, and then we will manifest the lack of love in intensity. This is the law using you.

If you consciously understand the momentum of the pendulum and you act, not react, you will have love and you will choose to learn from the lack of love in the way you choose to experience it. For instance, you can learn what it is you need to know about it by observing lack of love in the world, meditate on it, and decide and choose to learn the lessons this way, instead of creating a painful situation to experience in order to get the lesson and know the rhythm.

Like the ebb and flow of the oceans, you can get knocked around by the current because you are resisting or not being aware of the rhythm of the current or you flow with the current by choosing to go with the energies. Going with them is to know whatever occurs in life, we will experience the rhythm of the flow, both sides of it, of, so we choose how we ride that rhythm.

The Law of Rhythm is a Choice
Sink or Swim

If you stand in a current rigid and unwilling to flow or be flexible, then that current will wash you out or take you under. If you are willing to trust and to relax and go with the flow, you will ride to safety on the current.

Many times when we have an issue to work through or a lesson that has come up in our life and we stand rigid in the lesson, fighting the current. Look back on these moments, you have always experienced the opposite of that lesson, but you may have been slung into it like being shot from where you are to the other side of it like on a slingshot. If you consciously know you will want to learn the other side, you can use the law of rhythm to ride the wave there, go with the current and choose a gentler experience to learn it.

In order to move through these with rhythm and flow, you must have trust. Without trust, you will always focus on the negative side longer than you need to. It is a choice to be happy and trust that by knowing wonderful and great things are coming or choose to stay sad, angry, and unhappy. If you focus too long on the sad, anger or unhappiness, you remain there longer until you choose to learn from it and leave it. What your attention is on so is your intention.

Focus on what is present in your life right now. Focus on your hopes, desires, and dreams and then apply the concept of the law of rhythm to them. Knowing the rhythm is always occurring, look at how it is you are working with the law of rhythm. If things seem out of sorts right now or on the downswing of the pendulum, then focus on the good that is coming. The pendulum or your life MUST go on the upswing, as it is the law of rhythm.

Focus on the upswing coming after a downswing because it will happen. This process is to flow with the waves in your life. If you focus on how much things are NOT how you want them you are swimming upstream and fighting the current and then things will take longer to come in that are on the upswing. In doing this you will also feel as if you are sinking or being pulled out or under by the current.

Stop fighting it and CHOOSE to focus on the good that is coming! Know it has to come; it is the law of rhythm. The law of rhythm teaches us balance. As you learn from both sides of the experiences and master this law, you will know how to choose the balance.

Be Conscious of Where You Are at in Life
Know When You are Swimming With The Flow
or When You are Being Dragged Under

You must be able to identify when you are fighting the current and when you are flowing with it. Be conscious where your thoughts, feelings, and action/reactions are in every moment.

Everything is moving in perfect rhythm and in perfect speed, so if you feel hardship or stuck, you are fighting the current of the rhythm. Just as you cannot stop the seasons from happening, you cannot change the natural flow of the rhythm. You can, however, by being conscious, choose how you ride the current. If things are in a state of discomfort, you can focus on the good coming or you can fight the current by focusing on how bad things feel.

To focus on what is coming means you are saying, "Show me the lesson and assist me in riding the current by embracing this time and learning what I want to learn." You then will get to the outcome with ease of riding of the current. It ISN'T about saying, "Let me out of this rhythm by skipping over the experience." Instead, you are choosing to ride the experience differently.

You can spend time and energy fighting the rhythm by complaining about it and focusing on it being hard, uncomfortable, unfair, or negative, or you can focus on what good will come of it all by flowing with the lesson and looking at what you are experiencing as an opportunity to learn instead of an obstacle to get over.

If you learn to work with the law of rhythm, you will be riding the currents in no time instead of treading water and sinking under.

Law Eleven Exercises

Exercise One
Think back on lessons or experiences in life where you have been rigid and inflexible. Go back in your mind and see a different way you could have learned the lesson in more flow and rhythm.

Exercise Two
Go to the ocean and meditate with its rhythm and see how you feel and think. Let new insights come to you. If you are far from the ocean, get a tape of ocean sounds to create a similar experience.

Exercise Three
Pay attention to all rhythms occurring in your life now and assess the situations. Are you treading water or are you riding the currents?

List any places in your life that are not where you would like them to be – attitude, health, relationships, etc.

For those in which you feel you are treading water, meditate on the good that is coming and then ask what you are learning from this rhythm in your life now.

Exercise Four
Listen to different rhythms of music this week and FEEL them.

THE LAW OF GENDER

This law is rarely written about and just about never found in anything dealing with the law of attraction, yet it is as important as all twelve laws. This law shows us that all things are made up of male and female components. All things have a gestation period and this includes thoughts.

The law of gender states that every thought is a seed and seeds need to grow. When seeds grow, they need to take time and energy before it manifests into a plant. Our thoughts are spiritual seeds and they also need to be nurtured and take time to grow and manifest.

Like anything with male/female energy gestation must take place. It is much like the parable of the sower. He sowed the seeds and some fell on rocks and did not survive. Some fell in thorns and were choked. Others fell on the ground and birds found them and ate them. The ones that fell on fertile soil flourished and grew and came to fruition. This is a lot like many of our thoughts. Some make it and some don't but it is ultimately whether we plant them in fertile soil.

Many wonder how long it will take for their thoughts to manifest. As with anything worthwhile, it takes some time, every seed being different and unique, but all seeds manifest in their own perfect time.

Seed Your Dreams

Each one of your dreams is a seed being planted. Each dream (seed) needs your attention and your nurturing. There are many way to go about having your dreams come true, as there are also many ways we can stop them from happening.

The work, nurturing, and love of your dream (seed) will assist the seed to grow and manifest quicker. Daydream about your dreams, **FEEL** your dreams and what they would feel like once you had manifested them. How much time to spend thinking about bringing your dreams to fruition? If we work on taking care of our garden of dreams they will manifest in physical form. Plant your seeds in faith, hope, and trust and you will see them manifest.

Many people go about their day not truly believing their dreams will come true. In everyday chaos or turmoil, they can't see a way to the dream. Thoughts of "IF it happens" or "it looks so far away" or "I don't see a way to it," all stop the manifestation process. Each person must practice this and plant their seeds in the soil of faith, hope, and trust. When you do this, these dreams HAVE to grow.

KNOW Your Seeds Will Grow

Have you ever just had a strong feeling something will happen and then it did? That was the law of gender working. But if you have doubt, depression, or have lost faith, trust, and hope, nothing will happen for you.

Look at the law of gender as a strong knowing, just as if you know if you turn your faucet on water will come out of it. Take that feeling of just knowing that when you turn a faucet on water will flow from it and you will understand the law of gender. Actually, if you have ever turned the faucet on and it did not flow, you would be confused and shocked why it did not.

When you plant a seed of dreams and it has not manifested yet, take that feeling of just KNOWING the water will flow and apply it to your seed of dreams. Just know and FEEL the knowing as the water will flow from the faucet. In the same way, your dreams will manifest.

How Does the Law of Gender Work?

Use the following steps and you will find that the law of gender is at work here and it will become effortless to plant your garden and manifest its fruits.

1. Know that all your thoughts are spiritual seeds.

2. All seeds grow and manifest in exact correct timing.

3. Dreams always come true as long as you have faith, hope, and trust.

4. All seeds need attention, love and nurturing to manifest, if you switch your focus off of them, they stop growing.

5. Patience in your dreams keeps the growth happening, checking on them and digging them up will stunt their growth or kill them.

6. Don't just believe they will manifest, KNOW they will manifest as well as you know the water will flow from your faucet.

All dreams will manifest into the physical, for it's the law. Always know they will and never stop trusting.

Law Twelve Exercises

Exercise One
List the dreams that HAVE come true for you. Go back and remember how you felt before they came true. Were you certain they would happen? Did you have faith in these dreams?

Exercise Two
List all the dreams you have that have not happened yet and feel how you are inside with them.

- Are they farfetched of reaching?
- Do you doubt?
- Can you imagine living them?

Exercise Three
Take one of these dreams you feel has not manifested and meditate on it. See what comes up for you.

- Do you feel you truly want it?
- Do you feel deserving?
- Is it a farfetched idea for you?
- Do you lack trust?

If so, ask yourself why you don't trust the universe to take care of your needs.

Exercise Four
Rewrite and see your dreams in a different way until you feel certain they can manifest. Even if you have to change your dreams slightly, take one step closer to the dream, a baby step. As you see these smaller gains materialize, then take another dream step.

CONCLUSION

Each law is powerful, but when applied as a whole lifestyle, rather than individual laws, your whole world opens up. You are truly UNLIMITED – as you always have been and always will be.

Know that change begins within and it begins with YOU. Many people, especially now with all the change going on in the world, want to contribute and make positive change or heal their communities and others around the world. Know that as you change and heal, your frequency vibrates higher. This shift affects the whole world around you and the world around you begins to reflect what has evolved within your own consciousness. You can make an immense contribution to the awakening of the collective consciousness of the planet by living your truth and integrating all the Universal Laws in your life as they were meant to be.

Be patient with yourself while you learn to integrate these laws into your life. Even if you do not master them all in this lifetime, the more of them you learn to walk and live daily will make a huge and positive change in your life. It will just keep getting better.

It is as simple as being in the present moment, or what I like to say Live In The Everyday (L.I.T.E) with Universal Laws.

Thank you for sharing your radiant light and love with the world and I wish you the most joyful path for your Be-ing.

If you would like more information or enrichment on the twelve Universal Laws I offer several programs on integrating the laws into your daily living.

L.I.T.E.
Live In The Everyday with the 12 Universal Laws- learn how to apply the laws in the moment.

L.I.T.E. Within
Taking Universal Laws to the next level and integrating the sub-laws.

L.I.T.E. Transformation- Be the Change
This 2 day workshop is designed to assist you in staying in integrity with yourself and soul path and to understand the ethics involved with teaching and healing.

L.I.T.E.
Live In Truth Everyday- integrating the Universal Laws and sub-laws in specific areas of your life. This course puts you on the fast track to completely transform your life.

Anne Angelheart is available for private sessions, group teaching, experiential workshops, retreats, and ongoing mentoring.

www.anneangelheart.com

www.litecourse.com

Made in United States
North Haven, CT
13 December 2024